Food For Thought
Using Bowls For The Soul™

Food For Thought Using Bowls For The Soul™

NOURISHING YOUR MIND, BODY & SPIRIT

Wendy Sosik

HEART CHAKRA
press

USA
www.heartchakrapress.com

ISBN-13: 9780692771518
ISBN-10: 0692771514
Library of Congress Control Number: 2016913361
Heart Chakra Press, Sparta, NJ

Table of Contents

Preface

The idea for Bowls for the Soul™ came to me while working with Andy, a Reiki client and my friend's father. At eighty-five years of age, Andy's colon cancer had returned. While he was undergoing chemo treatments, I would go to his home and perform Reiki. (Reiki is an ancient Chinese energy healing technique used to release stresses in the body on a physical, mental, emotional, and cellular level.) He had not a clue what Reiki was, but he was open and went with it, and soon found he was sleeping much better and his appetite had improved after just a few sessions.

At the time, I didn't know he was also diabetic and wasn't eating nourishing foods. Since I understand the foods we eat are critical to healing the body, I decided to make him some homemade organic chicken soup for my next visit. This was when I first experienced my *a-ha!* design moment: I would create an affirmation bowl for him to eat his soup from. I designed the bowl to incorporate the seven main chakra energy points, each represented by their color along with corresponding affirmations for each. Thanks to my friend Christine, some paint, and a kiln, my design idea came to fruition. This bowl offers support for positive thinking and mindful eating—key ingredients to inner peace, healing, and overall wellness.

The affirmation bowl is a wonderful tool to help focus on positive thoughts and intentions especially important when dealing with an illness, which tends to magnify thoughts of fear and hopelessness. How you feel about your ability to recover and heal will have a direct impact on the process. Two people may have the same diagnosis and undergo the same treatment, but only one of them may recover and go on to live a healthy life. Why is this? Their personal belief system most likely played a role in their recovery outcome.

Introduction

Welcome, and congratulations on bringing this bowl into your realm! You just took a significant step in committing to making positive changes in your life. Being aware of what you think about and what you eat daily is empowering, and using your Bowl for the Soul™ has many benefits. The bowl was designed to support daily mindfulness and bring awareness to food portioning. This guide will help you better understand the influence of words on your mind, and the power of the mind over the body.

Your level of success is dependent on your ability to break old habits, change your belief systems, and take measurable actions to create new habits and beliefs. Purchasing this book is the first step in creating positive change in your life. To achieve success creating a healthier and happier you, you will need a sense of commitment, self-acceptance, and patience.

Accept where you are now and embrace it. Know that it is what it is, and you are in the process of creating a new reality for yourself. The pain we inflict on ourselves occurs most when we resist the circumstances that happen in our lives. Peace can only be found in pure acceptance of what is, so know in your heart you have all that you need WITHIN YOURSELF to create the life you desire. While this is all true, you must be aware: if you feel you are a victim of life's circumstances and feel you have no control over your life, you will not be empowered to shift your reality. It's critical to feel and know that you can create what you desire in this world. It all starts with our thoughts.

This book contains some basic concepts for consideration when learning to understand the mind-body connection. It also has guidelines for using the affirmation bowl for meditation and mindful eating. Once you understand the influences of the mind over the body, you can then work on shifting your thoughts and beliefs to change the state of your body to a healthier being. Bowls for the Soul™ is a tool created with love to support your journey to wholeness. Once you believe you're the creator of your reality and you accept anything is possible, it's critical to maintain that mindset for a period of time to achieve success. The best way to do this is to reinforce your new mindset on a daily basis. Our minds are not so quick to jump on board with change, and we will naturally have thoughts that will resist it. Use this bowl as a means to reprogram old beliefs into new ones that serve your wellness in mind, body, and spirit. You are more powerful than you ever suspected.

The Significance of the Shape of the Bowl and Placement of the Words

The shape of the bowl is similar to a cone, which in this case represents the expanse of the universe. The shape also represents your personal expanse and journey for greater self-awareness and greater consciousness. The deliberate placement of I AM is at the base of the bowl—the core, the heart center, the root connection to earth—and from that begins the rise of the journey represented by using the spiral formation of the affirmation words. Your journey (the spiral) not only rises up to higher consciousness, but it also expands and radiates outward to the universe. This represents your action to expand your personal journey to greater awareness of your physical, mental, emotional, and spiritual selves.

You (and the I AM) are at the bottom of the vessel, and as you read or speak each affirmation word on your journey, you rise to the top of the bowl. If you have food in the bowl, with each bite you become filled with the words and the bowl becomes lighter as it is emptied. Once the bowl is emptied entirely, you're completely full and you can then turn the bowl over for a moment. At this time, notice the I AM will be on top of the mountain, which will represent you being closer to your divine spiritual self. When our mind and body are filled with loving, kind intentions, we ascend to our true selves.

If you notice the placement of the words, you'll see how the words relate directly to the expanse of the bowl, which directly speaks to the growth and expanse of each one of us. Strong, secure, creative, well, empowered, and capable are relatively close to I AM. These are thoughts and feelings we develop from looking within ourselves, and we don't necessarily need others outside ourselves to attain these emotions. Notice how the loving, grateful, forgiving, calm, expressive, insightful, wise, connected, divine, and loved radiate farther and farther from the words I AM. Yes, we address these aspects within ourselves, as well; however, we absolutely need to reach out to others to expand and grow in these areas. I love that this bowl represents our personal and universal expansion in so many ways.

What's in an "I"?

The use of the serif style "I" on your Bowl for the Soul is intentional to represent all that you are. The "I" represents your authentic self, your divine nature. It makes a bold statement that you are strong, balanced, and solid. The lower horizontal line represents your grounding and connection to this physical world. The lower line radiates to the left and right, representing the infinite energetic expanse into the physical plain on earth. The horizontal line above represents your communication to your higher self, your spiritual self. The upper line on the letter radiates to the left and right, representing the infinite energetic expanse into the spiritual realm, your higher self. The vertical line connecting the upper realm and the lower one is representational of your authentic self. You are that vertical line connecting the two worlds. You are energetically connected and connecting the two worlds.

CHAPTER 1

The Mind-Body Connection
and the Power of Words

The Mind-Body Connection

First we must understand the power of the mind over the body and how they are innately connected. The thoughts we think, good or bad, affect our bodies. Most of us are not even aware of our thoughts; we go through our daily lives half asleep on autopilot. Our thoughts and how we see the world are based on our belief systems, and our belief systems are based on past experiences and social conditioning. It's important to understand that to change our thought patterns and create new and different outcomes, we have to pay attention to what we have been thinking that hasn't served us well. Only then can we make a conscious effort to create new beliefs and new thought patterns so they become permanent parts of our subconscious minds.

You have the power to CHOOSE what you think about! We have a choice, so why do we choose thoughts that don't serve us well? A few reasons: 1) we aren't aware of what we are thinking, 2) the thoughts are comfortable and familiar, and 3), the thoughts are ingrained into our belief systems. However, we have the power within us to shift that and focus on only the thoughts that support our well-being.

Since stress in our mind is the number one cause for "dis-ease" in the body, we can easily recognize the importance of meditation and creating mental peace for ourselves. We can make this shift with meditation and using positive affirmations to reshape our mental states of mind. When we learn to be the observers of our thoughts, and disconnect from the emotions they present, we then can begin to make some real changes in our lives. The observer has the power to choose the thoughts that support us and let go of the ones that do not.

The Power of Words

Words are very powerful. Words can cut us like knives and make us feel incredibly deep pain. Words can support us and create peace, joy, and love. Choose your words wisely; they have a lasting impact on others in ways you may never know. I'm sure you can think of a time when a family member, friend, or colleague used unkind words that struck you to the core. To think it in your head is one thing, to say it is another. Don't say it if it is hurtful; you can't take it back once it's out of your mouth.

We recognize the importance of words in our daily life. Using this bowl is like having a life coach in your home prompting you to make wise choices to support your overall health. This is a simple step-by-step guide for different techniques you can put into action. I encourage you to also create your own technique for using the bowl. We are all unique beings, and what resonates for one person may not for another.

Feel free to share your technique here www.bowlsforthesoul.com.

CHAPTER 2

Food for Thought ~ Mindful Eating & Portioning

Mindfully eating from the bowl is a wonderful way to keep your mind, body, and spirit in the moment. Use this basic food portion guideline as a reference. What follows are two different versions as well as food for thought to support your success.

Version 1. Eat Anything

Nourish Your Mind, Body & Spirit With The Power Of Portion Control...

Use your Affirmation Bowl as support for healthy eating by following the food portion guideline. The portion should be below the recommended affirmation words for that food.

Salad Greens – Connected... Divine... LOVED

Clear Soup, Broth – Insightful...Wise

Popcorn – Calm... Expressive

Green Vegetables – Loving... Grateful... Forgiving

Vegetables – Empowered... Capable

Meat, Seafood, Fruit – Creative... Well

Ice Cream, Potatoes, Pasta, Rice – Strong... Secure

Nourish Your Mind, Body & Spirit with the Power of Portion Control...

Use your Affirmation Bowl as support for healthy eating by following this food portion guideline. The portion should be below the recommended affirmation words for that food.

Salad Greens—Connected... Divine... LOVED

Clear Soup, Broth—Insightful...Wise

Popcorn —Calm... Expressive

Green Vegetables—Loving... Grateful... Forgiving

Vegetables —Empowered... Capable

Meat, Seafood, Fruit —Creative... Well

Ice Cream, Potatoes, Pasta, Rice—Strong... Secure

This first version is the food portion guide for eating *any* food in moderation. Portion control is really key. This is the "Weight Watchers" approach to food. Of course, it's always a good idea to keep the consumption of processed and fried foods to a minimum.

Healthy Eating Tips:

* Do not skip breakfast.
* Do not eat any food past 7:00 p.m.
* Be mindful of your intake of sugar, carbohydrates, protein, and fats.
* Eat smaller meals every 2½ to 3 hours to keep up your metabolism.
* Hydrate, hydrate, hydrate (half your body weight in ounces of water every day).
* Use a food journal to bring awareness to your eating habits.

Version 2. Eating Clean

Nourish Your Mind, Body & Spirit With The Power Of Portion Control...

Use your Affirmation Bowl as support for healthy eating by following the food portion guideline. The portion should be below the recommended affirmation words for that food.

Leafy Greens – Connected... Divine... LOVED _____

Clear Soups, Broth – Insightful...Wise _____

Stews, Kale Chips – Calm... Expressive

Colorful Vegetables – Loving... Grateful... Forgiving _____

Rooted Vegetables – Empowered... Capable _____

Lean Proteins – Creative... Well _____

Whole Grains – Strong... Secure _____

Nourish Your Mind, Body & Spirit with the Power of Portion Control...

Use your Affirmation Bowl as support for healthy eating by following this food portion guideline. The portion should be below the recommended affirmation words for that food.

Leafy Greens—Connected... Divine... LOVED

Clear Soups, Broth—Insightful...Wise

Stews, Kale Chips—Calm... Expressive

Colorful Vegetables—Loving... Grateful... Forgiving

Rooted Vegetables—Empowered... Capable

Lean Proteins—Creative... Well

Whole Grains—Strong... Secure

The second version is the food portion guide for eating clean. What is "eating clean"? The general guideline for "clean eating" is consuming food that comes directly from the earth and is not processed or is minimally processed. When eating clean, you don't eat foods that have more than six ingredients listed on the box and you don't eat white starch or sugars. Eat organic foods as much as possible, especially dairy, berries, apples, and soy products.

Healthy Eating Tips:

* Read all food package labels; six ingredients or less is best.
* Buy organic dairy products: milk, cheese, yogurt, eggs, etc.
* Buy organic fruits and vegetables, thin-skinned especially (e.g., apples, pears, grapes, all berries).
* Buy organic grass-fed beef, chicken, or turkey.
* Frozen vegetables and fruit are healthier than canned foods.

I can't stress this enough: WE ARE WHAT WE EAT. Your body and mind will not feel good if the fuel you are putting into your body is junk. If you want to be a lean, mean, fit machine, you need to EAT CLEAN! You do NOT put low-grade fuel in a Ferrari and expect it to run at peak performance. It requires high-grade fuel. Same for you! You will not feel good if you are eating Doritos and drinking soda every day.

When it comes to our relationship with food, we need to consider many factors. Many of us are emotional eaters; we reach for food to help us feel better in times of stress or when we are upset. We also reach for those treats as rewards or to celebrate—"Great game! Let's get ice cream." Substitute that behavior with a healthier, more supportive response. Go for a walk or stretch, meditate, talk to a friend.

Occasionally—meaning once a month, not every week—have a small ice cream cone with only one topping (kid-sized would be ideal).

Some of us carry the mindset of "live to eat" instead of "eat to live." I can guarantee the "live to eat" individuals are the ones more likely to carry extra weight. When you become more mindful of your body and more aware of how you feel in your mind and body when you eat different foods, you will start to make better choices. You will no longer feel tired, sluggish, or moody from excessive carbs, fats, and sugar highs and lows.

Also, many of us don't LOVE our physical bodies. We don't fully accept and appreciate our bodies as they currently are, and it's hard for us to be supportive of something we don't love. If we don't love our body, why would we want to take care of it? (It would be much easier for us to have the fit, lean body first to support and maintain than it would be to support ourselves hoping we will one day get to where we want to be.) Here's the thing: it's the only body you will ever have! Your body is what's sustaining you in this world. The condition of your body is what will determine how long you will live on this earth; it will determine the quality of your life. Are you able to pursue your dreams or do you have physical limitations that impact how you are dealing with them? The sooner you recognize those limitations, the better, because you are then capable of changing your lifestyle to a healthier one.

We need to fall in love with our bodies. I encourage you to spend time on a daily basis focusing on the parts of your body that you like and/ or love. If this is a challenge, focus on the amazing things your body is capable of doing. Focus on the constants: your heartbeat (amazing how it regulates the flow of blood throughout your entire body) or your liver (which filters out impurities), the digestive process, the movement of your hands and fingers, etc. Your body truly is a masterpiece; you'll experience a sense of wonderment when you take time to be aware of the way it functions.

CHAPTER 3
Simple Mindful Meditations

Method #1 Mindful Eating & Portioning

Fill your bowl with high-quality fuel for nourishment, such as healthy soup, oatmeal, salad, veggies, or yogurt. Take note of the words that are visible once you place the food in the bowl. Connect with each word: state the words I AM, followed by each affirmation word you see. Take note of the colors of the words. How do the colors make you feel? How do the words make you feel? As you mindfully take food out of the bowl with your spoon or fork and bring it to your mouth, visualize all the words are infused into the food. Feel the power of the affirmations as though you are ingesting these positive, supportive words and bring them into your core, your soul being.

Can you feel yourself connecting to each affirmation word? Can you feel your soul filling up with these words of empowerment? Your being is literally each one of these words in the bowl. You have to believe it, know it, be convinced it is no other way, and then you will feel the inner connection to each word and truly own it. When you finish the food in the bowl, you will see the words I AM every time. This is the confirmation of your power.

What a great way to start the day! It's like having an empowerment coach right there with you at every meal. This is a great meditation tool for those who find sitting still and quieting the mind for a period of time too challenging. By using The Bowl, you will be quieting the ego chatter and connecting to the inner voice from your soul.

Method #2 Bowl Used for Meditation Only ~ No Food in the Bowl

Before we begin any meditation, we want to clear the mind and body of any stressors we may be holding onto. Do this by taking a cleansing breath in through your nose and exhaling any stress in your mind and body out through your mouth. Repeat this process three times before you begin the bowl meditations.

Place the bowl in your hands and look at the words I AM at the bottom of the bowl. Take a breath in and, at the same time, state I AM, either in your head or aloud. Take another breath in, say I AM in your mind or aloud, and look at the first word at the bottom of the bowl. On your exhalation, state the word STRONG. Breathe in the words I AM, and exhale the next word SECURE. Continue this exercise for all the words in the bowl, and especially the last word, LOVED.

While you mindfully breathe in and out stating the affirmations, it's also important to *feel* each affirmation word. Are you able to feel yourself being strong and secure? Take note if you are not in sync with the affirmation word. This could mean something is bothering you, perhaps subconsciously, and should be addressed and looked at more closely. Ask yourself, "Why is it that I don't feel strong? Why do I see myself as weak? Is that a belief I adopted early in my life? In which examples from my life do I recognize my strength?" Focus on those instances in your life where you recognize your strength. This will help you to shift from weak to strong. Until that shift, you won't be able to fully step into your power.

Method #3 Bowl Used Visually for Chakra Energy Healing Meditation ~ Holding the Bowl

Each affirmation word was carefully chosen to represent an affirmative statement that resonates with each of the seven main chakra energy points in the body. In yoga, the word *chakra* refers to any physical or spiritual energy centers in our body, especially one of the seven centers that are aligned with the spinal column. Its origin is Sanskrit and means "wheel" or "circle." The words are also painted in the corresponding color to each chakra energy center. Visually, you can use the colors for meditation to heal each of the chakra energy centers located in the body. Refer to the two Chakra Color Charts that follow.

Chakra Color Chart with Corresponding Affirmation Words

Nourish Your Mind, Body & Spirit With The Power Of Words...

Say: "I AM" and then recite the affirmation words in the bowl. Saying, visualizing and feeling each affirmation word will help bring you closer to well-being.

Chakra – Affirmations

Crown – Connected... Divine
Third Eye – Insightful... Wise
Throat – Calm... Expressive
Heart – Loving...Grateful... Forgiving
Solar Plexus – Empowered... Capable
Sacral – Creative... Well
Root – Strong... Secure

Nourish Your Mind, Body & Spirit with the Power of Words...

Say: "I AM" and then recite the affirmation words in the bowl. Saying, visualizing, and feeling each affirmation word will help bring you closer to well-being.

Chakra—Affirmations

Crown—Connected... Divine

Third Eye—Insightful...Wise

Throat —Calm... Expressive

Heart—Loving...Grateful...Forgiving

Solar Plexus—Empowered... Capable

Sacral—Creative... Well

Root—Strong... Secure

Chakra Location in the Body with Corresponding Colors

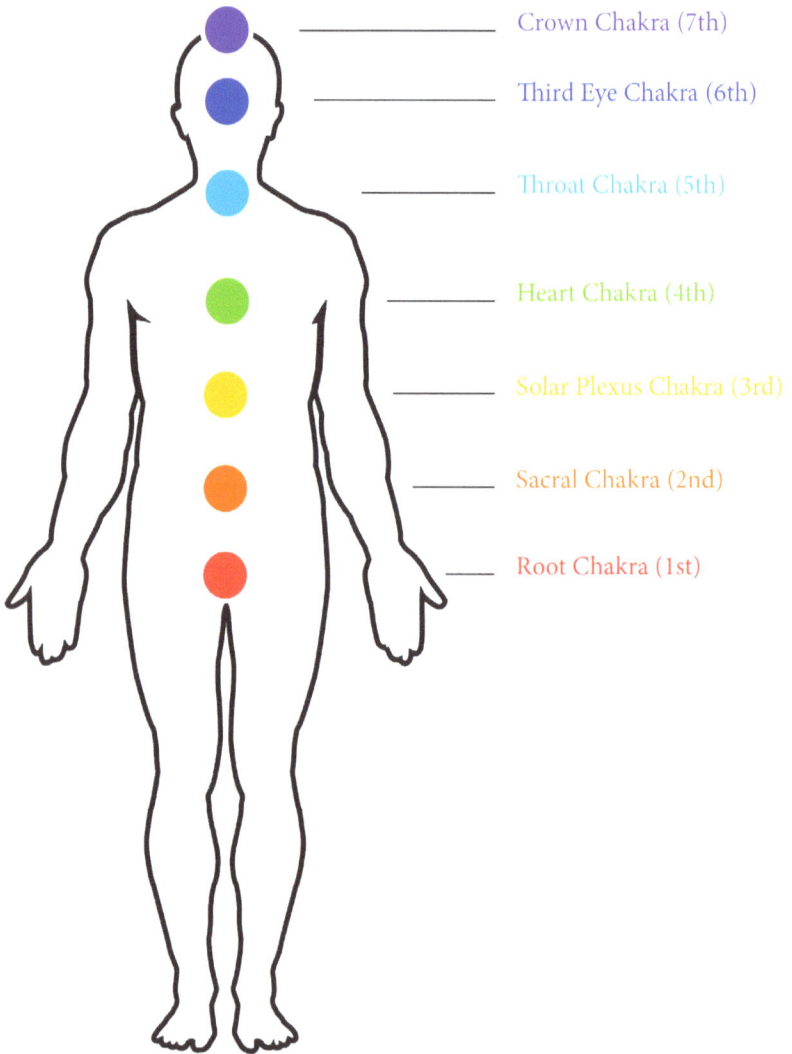

_____ Crown Chakra (7th)

_____ Third Eye Chakra (6th)

_____ Throat Chakra (5th)

_____ Heart Chakra (4th)

_____ Solar Plexus Chakra (3rd)

_____ Sacral Chakra (2nd)

_____ Root Chakra (1st)

Visual Meditation While Holding the Bowl

The bowl can be used to bring in healing energy to each of the seven main chakra energy points in the body. Hold the bowl in the palm of your hands and focus your attention on one color of the affirmation words.

Start with *Strong…Secure*. They are both red. Look at the two red words and visualize you are bringing the color red to your root chakra at the base of your spine.

Continue by turning the bowl so you can read the orange words *Creative…Well*. Bring the orange color to your sacral chakra just above the root chakra near your navel.

Turn the bowl again so you see the words *Empowered…Capable* in yellow. Bring that color to your solar plexus chakra, located about two inches above your navel area.

Turn bowl to the three words *Loving…Grateful…Forgiving* in green. Bring that color to your heart chakra, located where you heart is in the center of your chest.

Next is *Calm…Expressive* in blue. Bring the color blue to your throat chakra, located at your throat.

Insightful…Wise are indigo. Bring this color to your third eye chakra, located in the middle of your brow between your eyes.

Next is the color violet *Connected…Divine…LOVED*. Visualize you are bringing in the color violet to your crown chakra, which is located on the top of your head in the center. This is your connection to your higher self.

Once you have visually brought in all seven colors to their corresponding chakra energy points in your body, take a moment to visualize the seven colors placed in the center meridian of your body, beginning at the top of your head and ending at the base of your spine. Take a few mindful breaths, feeling the warmth and energy of each color in each location in your body.

Method #4 Bowl Used with Food for Chakra Energy Healing Meditation ~ Eating from the Bowl

Visual Meditation While Eating from the Bowl

Using the affirmation bowl with food to bring in healing energy to each of the seven main chakra points is a fun, effective technique. First, place healthy food with the corresponding healthy portion into the bowl. Visualize all the colors in the bowl are transfused into the food you are about to eat. There is a reason we begin at the bottom of the bowl and work our way up to the top. To reach the state of connectedness, divinity, and love, we need to start with a solid foundation to support our personal growth. So although you see the words that spiral around the upper portion of the bowl, know those are what you are aspiring to, however there is work to be done below the surface (hiding by the foods placed in the bowl). Perhaps the food represents the work, and as you use energy to feed yourself from this bowl, you are taking action to nourish yourself and uncover the attributes that are innately yours.

When you take your first bite, focus on the words painted red, *Strong...Secure*. Imagine the color red is swallowed, travels down your throat to your stomach, and moves down inside your body to settle in the root chakra at the base of your spine.

Continue with the orange words *Creative... Well*. As you swallow, feel the energy of the orange color traveling down inside your body to the sacral chakra point just above the root chakra below the navel.

Next are the words *Empowered... Capable* in yellow. Bring the yellow energy to your solar plexus approximately two inches above your navel.

Loving... Grateful... Forgiving are representing the heart chakra with the color green. Bring the green healing heart energy to your heart chakra, located in the center of your chest.

Blue represents the throat chakra with the words *Calm... Expressive*. Focus this energy coming into your throat area.

The color indigo represents *Insightful... Wise*. Visualize, as you bring the food into your mouth, you are sending the indigo color up to your third eye energy point, located in the middle of your brow between your eyes.

Last is the color violet, which represents *Connected... Divine... LOVED*. Visualize you are bringing in the color violet to your crown chakra, which is located on the top of your head in the center. This is your connection to your higher self.

Do this until you have moved through all seven chakra colors using the Chakra Color Chart that follows.

Chakra Location in the Body with Corresponding Colors

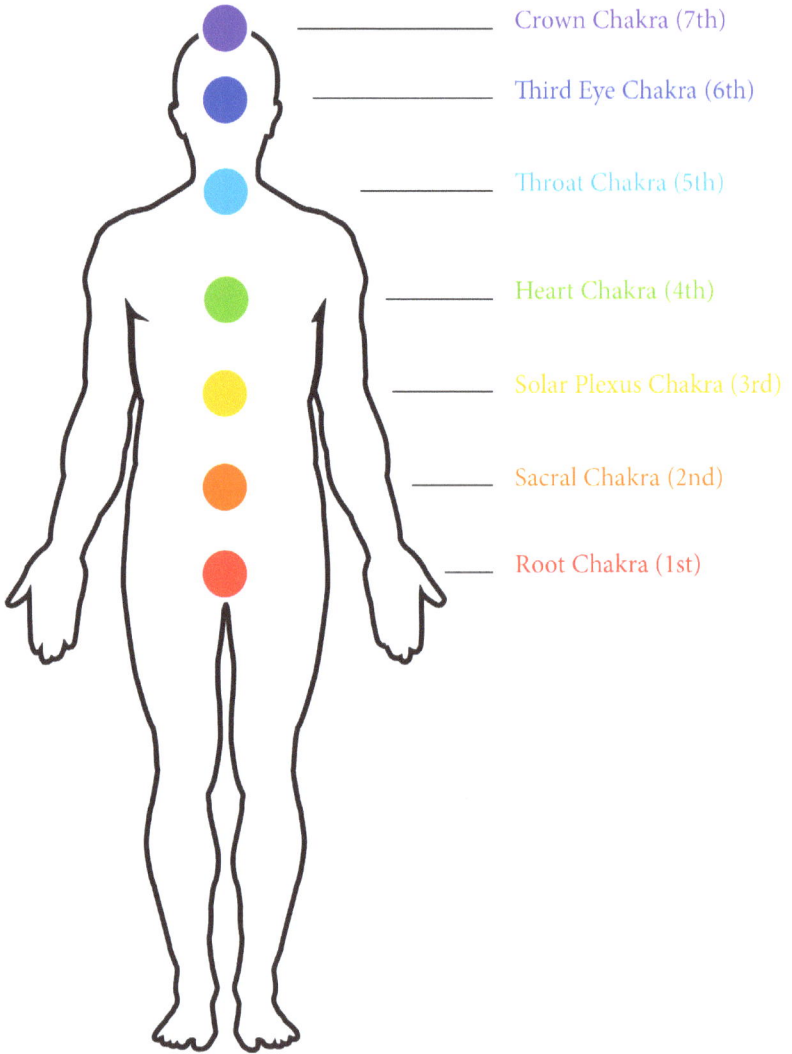

Crown Chakra (7th)

Third Eye Chakra (6th)

Throat Chakra (5th)

Heart Chakra (4th)

Solar Plexus Chakra (3rd)

Sacral Chakra (2nd)

Root Chakra (1st)

Root Chakra – Red – Strong, Secure

Sacral Chakra – Orange – Creative, Well

Solar Plexus Chakra – Yellow – Empowered, Capable

Heart Chakra – Green – Loving, Grateful, Forgiving

Throat Chakra – Blue – Calm, Expressive

Third Eye Chakra – Indigo – Insightful, Wise

Crown Chakra – Violet – Connected, Divine, LOVED! YES YOU ARE!

I AM – The Most Powerful Declaration Used to Create Your Life

Method #5 Meditation While Handwashing the Bowl

While you are handwashing the bowl, focus your attention on the words in the bowl. Either aloud or in your mind, start with the words "I AM" and read each of the words as they spiral up the inside of the bowl. Use this practice as a daily declaration to help you stay focused on your self love and healing. You can also elaborate on this by asking yourself, "How am I Strong?" and answering with an example that is true for you. "I AM strong …" Do this with each of the words in the bowl. This is a powerful tool for you to tap into understanding what your beliefs are about yourself. I encourage you to do this exercise every time you eat from your bowl, which could be multiple times a day. You can also create your own meditation while handwashing the bowl and share it with others here: **www.bowlsforthesoul.com**.

CHAPTER 4

Advanced Mindful Meditations

Method #1 Infinity Seven Chakra Meditation

Begin by visualizing you are standing inside the center of the bowl on top of the words I AM.

Slowly imagine turning your body clockwise, looking at the words that start at the bottom of the bowl: *Strong...Secure*. Read each word as it spirals up the inside of the bowl. Finishing the meditation with the words **Connected**, **Divine**, and **Loved**.

Bring your attention the red words **Strong** and **Secure**, representing the root chakra energy at the bottom of the bowl. Visualize those words in red are moving in a figure-eight formation similar to the infinity symbol. Bring those words into you root chakra energy center through the front of your body and envision exit through the back of your body, forming an infinite loop. The loop intersects in the middle of the energy point. Continue this visualization for at least one minute and feel the power of each word as it moves through your energy center.

Next bring your awareness to your sacral chakra energy center, represented by the color orange. Visualize the orange words **Creative** and **Well** are moving in a figure-eight formation similar to the infinity symbol. Bring those words into your sacral chakra energy center through the front of your body and envision them exit through the back of your body, forming an infinite loop. The loop intersects in the middle of the energy point. Continue this visualization for at least one minute and feel the power of each word as it moves through your energy center.

Next bring your awareness to your solar plexus chakra energy center represented by the color yellow. Visualize the yellow words **Empowered** and **Capable** are moving in a figure-eight formation similar to the infinity symbol. Bring those words into your solar plexus chakra energy center through the front of your body and envision them exit through the back of your body, forming an infinite loop. The loop intersects in the middle of the energy point. Continue this visualization for at least one minute and feel the power of each word as it moves through your energy center.

Next bring your awareness to your heart chakra energy center represented by the color green. Visualize the green words **Loving**, **Grateful**, and **Forgiving** are moving in a figure-eight formation similar to the infinity symbol. Bring those words into your heart chakra energy center through the front of your body and envision them exit through the back of your body, forming an infinite loop. The loop intersects in the middle of the energy point. Continue this visualization for at least one minute and feel the power of each word as it moves through your energy center.

Next bring your awareness to your throat chakra energy center represented by the color blue. Visualize the blue words **Calm** and **Expressive** are moving in a figure-eight formation similar to the infinity symbol. Bring those words into your throat chakra energy center through the front of your body and envision them exit through the back of your body, forming an infinite loop. The loop intersects in the middle of the energy point. Continue this visualization for at least one minute and feel the power of each word as it moves through your energy center.

Next bring your awareness to your third eye chakra energy center represented by the color indigo. Visualize the indigo words **Insightful** and **Wise** are moving in a figure-eight formation similar to the infinity symbol. Bring those words into your third eye chakra energy center through the front of your body and envision them exit through the back of your body, forming an infinite loop. The loop intersects in the middle of the energy point. Continue this visualization for at least one minute and feel the power of each word as it moves through your energy center.

Next bring your awareness to your crown chakra energy center represented by the color violet. Visualize the violet words **Connected**, **Divine**, and **Loved** are moving in a figure-eight formation similar to the infinity symbol. Bring those words into your crown chakra energy center through the front of your body and envision them exit through the back of your body, forming an infinite loop. The loop intersects in the middle of the energy point. Continue this visualization for at least one minute and feel the power of each word as it moves through your energy center.

Return to visualizing yourself standing in the center of the bowl on top of the words I AM. Visualize the rainbow colors of the words are swirling around you and then enter through the top of your head, down through the center of your body, exiting through the souls of your feet and rising back up to surround your body like a protective bubble of wholeness. Feel that you are empowered and living in the truth of each of the affirmation words. Hold this feeling. When you are ready, bring your awareness back to the room.

Method #2 Radiating Ring Chakra Meditation

Begin by visualizing you are standing inside the center of the bowl on top of the words I AM.

Slowly imagine turning your body clockwise and look at the words that start at the bottom of the bowl: **Strong** and **Secure**. Read each word as it spirals up the inside the bowl.

Strong, Secure, Creative, Well, Empowered, Capable, Loving, Grateful, Forgiving, Calm, Expressive, Insightful, Wise, Connected, Divine, Loved.

Visualize the red words **Strong** and **Secure** are moving in a clockwise circular motion within your first energy center, the root chakra. As you hold those words, visualize they gradually move farther away from the energy center. Hold the words moving around your body in the root chakra area about eight feet away from your body. Expand the red energy affirmation circle out into the infinite universe, and then let it go.

Next, visualize the orange words **Creative** and **Well** are moving in a clockwise circular motion within your second energy center, the sacral chakra. As you hold those words, visualize they gradually move farther away from the energy center. Hold the words moving around your body in the sacral chakra area about eight feet away from your body. Expand the orange energy affirmation circle out into the infinite universe, and then let it go.

Next, visualize the yellow words **Empowered** and **Capable** are moving in a clockwise circular motion within your third energy center, the solar plexus chakra. As you hold those words, visualize they gradually move farther away from the energy center. Hold the words moving around your body in the solar plexus chakra area about eight feet away from your body. Expand the yellow energy affirmation circle out into the infinite universe, and then let it go.

Next, visualize the green words **Loving**, **Grateful**, and **Forgiving** are moving in a clockwise circular motion within your fourth energy center, the heart chakra. As you hold those words, visualize they gradually move farther away from the energy center. Hold the words moving around your body in the heart chakra area about eight feet away from your body. Expand the green energy affirmation circle out into the infinite universe, and then let it go.

Next, visualize the blue words **Calm** and **Expressive** are moving in a clockwise circular motion within your fourth energy center, the throat chakra. As you hold those words, visualize they gradually move farther away from the energy center. Hold the words moving around your body in the throat chakra area about eight feet away from your body. Expand the blue energy affirmation circle out into the infinite universe, and then let it go.

Next, visualize the indigo words **Insightful** and **Wise** are moving in a clockwise circular motion within your fifth energy center, the third eye chakra. As you hold those words, visualize they gradually move farther away from the energy center. Hold the words moving around your body in the third eye chakra area about eight feet away from your body. Expand the indigo energy affirmation circle out into the infinite universe, and then let it go.

Next, visualize the violet words **Connected**, **Divine**, and **Loved** are moving in a clockwise circular motion within your sixth energy center, the crown chakra. As you hold those words, visualize they gradually move farther away from the energy center. Hold the words moving around your body in the crown chakra area about eight feet away from your body. Expand the violet energy affirmation circle out into the infinite universe, and then let it go.

Close the meditation by bringing your awareness back to standing in the center of the bowl on top of the words I AM.

Visualize all the colors from inside the bowl containing the affirmation words are simultaneously spinning from within your energy centers out to your auric field. Hold this visual and know you are whole. Then release the energy into the universe. When you are ready, bring your awareness back to the room.

CHAPTER 5

Display, Share & Care for your Bowls
for the Soul™

Display Your Bowl

Display your affirmation bowl when not in use. Place your bowl in a
stand on the kitchen counter, table, mantle, or even on your night-
stand. It will remind you and your family throughout the day of these
powerful affirmation words that speak to your soul.

Seeing these words throughout the day will help reinforce positive
thoughts in your mind and quiet the negative chatter. Looking at the
colors in the bowls, which are similar to a rainbow, will help you connect to that inner child—your lighter side—and open up and connect
to your soul. As you glance at the bowl, check in with your gut and see
how you are feeling at the moment. If you sense you are deficient in
any affirmation word, bring it into your mind and body. Do a quick
meditation to pull in the energy of that word and/or the color to the
corresponding chakra point.

Share Your Bowl

By displaying your bowl in your home or office, you will be planting a seed of consciousness for growth and expansion in your community. When a family, friend, colleague, or client asks you about your Bowl for the Soul™ or comments on how cool it looks, this is your opportunity to ask if they are familiar with the concepts of affirmations and mindfulness—and maybe even dare to mention the chakra energy centers in our body.

You don't really know how you can impact someone's life. I learned the simplest actions can make the biggest change. Being your authentic self assures your inner light will shine through and touch others in a positive way. So shine on!

Care for Your Bowl

This affirmation bowl is created with loving intention, so it deserves the same loving energy when caring for it. While you are at the kitchen sink, handwashing your bowl, I encourage you to take this opportunity to be in the moment. Be one with the bowl. Wash it with loving intention—not thinking of what happened yesterday, or what you have to do later. The more time we spend *just being*, the less stressed you will be. How you care for the bowl can be a direct reflection on how you care for yourself. This is a perfect opportunity to make the commitment to love yourself just a little more.

CHAPTER 6

Words Defined: Definition of Affirmation Words

STRONG

*   Having, showing, or able to exert great bodily or muscular power;
*   Physically vigorous or robust;
*   Mentally powerful or vigorous;
*   Especially able, competent, or powerful in a specific field or respect;
*   Of great moral power, firmness, or courage.

SECURE

*   Free from or not exposed to danger or harm; safe;
*   Dependable; firm; not liable to fail, yield, become displaced, etc., as a support or a fastening; affording safety, as a place, in safe custody or keeping;
*   Free from care; without anxiety; emotionally secure.

CREATIVE

* Having the quality or power of creating;

* Resulting from originality of thought, expression, etc.; imaginative, originative; productive;

* To cause to come into being, as something unique that would not naturally evolve or that is not made by ordinary processes;

* To evolve from one's own thought or imagination, as a work of art or an invention.

WELL

* In a good or satisfactory manner, as though business is going well;

* Thoroughly, carefully, or soundly: to shake well before using; listen well;

* In a moral or proper manner: to behave well;

* Well-ness commendably, meritoriously, or excellently the quality or state of being healthy in body and mind, especially as the result of deliberate effort;

* An approach to healthcare that emphasizes preventing illness and prolonging life, as opposed to emphasizing treating diseases.

EMPOWERED

* To give power or authority to; authorize; to enable or permit.

CAPABLE

* Having power and ability; efficient; competent;
* Capable of, having the ability or capacity for, open to the influence or effect of.

LOVING

* Feeling or showing love; warmly affectionate; fond.

GRATEFUL

* Warmly or deeply appreciative of kindness or benefits received; thankful;
* Expressing or actuated by gratitude, pleasing to the mind or senses; agreeable or welcome; refreshing.

FORGIVING

* To grant pardon for or remission of (an offense, debt, etc.); absolve;
* To give up all claim on account of; remit (a debt, obligation, etc.);
* To grant pardon to (a person);
* To cease to feel resentment against: to forgive one's enemies;
* To cancel an indebtedness or liability of.

CALM

* Free from excitement or passion; tranquil: a calm face; a calm manner;

* Freedom from motion or disturbance; stillness;

* Freedom from agitation, excitement, or passion; tranquility; serenity.

EXPRESSIVE

* Full of expression; meaningful;

* Serving to express; indicative of power to express;

* Of, pertaining to, or concerned with expression;

* To put (thought) into words; utter or state;

* To show, manifest, or reveal: to express one's anger;

* To set forth the opinions, feelings, etc., of (oneself), as in speaking, writing, or painting;

* Insightful;

* An instance of apprehending the true nature of a thing, especially through intuitive understanding;

* Penetrating mental vision or discernment; faculty of seeing into inner character or underlying truth;

* An understanding of the motivational forces behind one's actions, thoughts, or behavior; self-knowledge.

WISE

* Having the power of discerning and judging properly as to what is true or right; possessing discernment, judgment, or discretion;

* Characterized by or showing such power; judicious or prudent: a wise decision.

CONNECTED

* United, joined, or linked;
* Having a connection;
* Joined together in sequence; linked coherently: connected ideas;
* Related by family ties;
* Having social or professional relationships, especially with influential or powerful persons;
* To cause to be associated, as in a personal or business relationship: to connect oneself with a group of like-minded persons;
* To associate mentally or emotionally.

DIVINE

* Of or pertaining to a god, especially the Supreme Being;
* Addressed, appropriated, or devoted to a god; religious; sacred: divine worship;
* Proceeding from a god: divine laws;
* Godlike; characteristic of or befitting a deity: divine magnanimity;
* Heavenly; celestial: the divine kingdom;
* The spiritual aspect of humans; the group of attributes and qualities of humankind regarded as godly or godlike.

LOVED

* Held in deep affection; cherished.

CHAPTER 7

Teaching Guide for Parents: Engaging
Questions to Stimulate Awareness,
Acceptance & Empowerment

The overall concept is that you are everything in this bowl—all of the affirmation words and colors represent our wholeness. Like a rainbow, we are a full spectrum of colors and energy. Looking at the many colors in the design reminds us to lighten up and to be more playful. As we grow older, we move away from our inner child and oftentimes get caught up in the heaviness of living in a world that creates fear, worry, and a sense of isolation.

This affirmation bowl can be used as tool to connect to your child with dialogue. It also helps empower them to learn that they posses the trait of each affirmation word in the bowl.

Since repetition is key to learning, using the bowl daily and displaying the bowl when not in use can be effective tools to reinforce a positive mindset in the family.

Words:

* Use the definition guide to discuss the meaning of each affirmation word with children. See page 26 for definitions

* Ask what their definition of the word is. If they don't know, give them an example of what the word means. Use them in the example.

* Pick one word for the day. Discuss the meaning and importance of the word and have each family member come up with an example of how it relates to them.

* Have your family members or friends give an example of how they see you being that particular affirmation statement (e.g., strong, wise, etc.). This can give you great insight on how others perceive you.

Colors:

* Talk about how all the different colors in the bowl represent the colors of the rainbow.

* Ask your child how they are like a rainbow.

* Ask how each color makes them feel. And why.

* Ask what comes to their mind when they think of each color.

* Have your child find something in nature that is represented by each color. This will help them to be more aware and connected to nature. When they're observing a sunset, sunrise, blossoms on a tree, a bird perched on a branch, etc., they are being in the moment and connecting to nature.

* Ask your child if each color represented their favorite food, what would it be?

* Name a favorite fruit for each color in the bowl.

* Name a favorite vegetable for each color in the bowl.

* Ask your child what they like that is each color.

* Name a person, place, or thing for each color in the bowl. If you ask them to name a favorite person, place, or thing, it will focus them on the positives of what they like.

SUGGESTED READING

The Four Agreements by Don Miguel Ruiz

The Alchemist by Paulo Coelho

Dying To Be Me by Anita Moorjani

A New Earth by Eckhart Tolle

Breaking the Habit of Being Yourself by Dr. Joe Dispenza

The Placebo Effect by Dr. Joe Dispenza

The Untethered Soul by Michael A. Singer

Power vs. Force by David R. Hawkins

Wheels of Life by Anodea Judith

The Eat-Clean Diet by Tosca Reno

The Conscious Parent by Dr. Shefali Tsabary

The Gifts of Imperfection by Brené Brown

Daring Greatly by Brené Brown

TESTIMONIALS

"I keep my affirmation bowl in my office and look at it often throughout the day. Each time I read the I AM statements, it elevates my energy to a place where I can enjoy more confidence and freedom to be myself. The self that I desire to be, all that is written on the bowl. Creating an environment that encourages a positive mindset enables me to add value to everyone I connect with. I am grateful for the bowl and highly recommend everyone get one."

—Angela Kubisky

*   *   *

"Whether you are just beginning your journey of well-being or further down your path, Bowls for the Soul™ are a must have tool. These bowls are more than a vessel to have a meal in. Your eyes are automatically drawn into the beautiful-colored lettering, compelling you to read the positive affirmations within the bowl. With each use you are gently retraining your brain to believe these bettering messages.

"We become what we tell ourselves we are. What an easy, beautiful way to feel good about yourself. Our family LOVES and uses our Bowls for the Soul™ every day. I found the companion guidebook vital in utilizing the full potential of these wonderful meditation bowls and was glad I ordered it."

—Lisa Kisch

*   *   *

"When I first saw the bowl, I knew I had to have it! I love the I AM, the words, and I love the concept. It's a light opening moment every time I use it."

—Alissa Okrent

"The bowl helps me to keep in mind the present moment and positivity."

—W. Miller

*   *   *

"I love my Bowl for the Soul™. I gravitate towards anything that nourishes the soul and this bowl immediately caught my eye when I met Wendy at a Mind/Body/Spirit fair booth. It is such a simple, positive addition to my life with its fun colors and meaningful message to instill awareness and positive intentions. Great gift idea for friends and family who are on the path or on the verge of awakening. I love it!!!"

—L. Parker

*   *   *

"I own one of the very meaningful and beautiful Bowls for the Soul™. The affirmation words painted simplistically around the circumference of the bowl allow me to achieve a more positive sense even when the day has been very long and filled with stress."

—Sue Rosenthal

ACKNOWLEDGMENTS

Thank you, Andy, for being the spark that brought to light the creation of Bowls For The Soul™. Many thanks to my supportive family.

And special thanks to my dear friend Christine Willis, who brought my design to fruition with her skilled, steady hand, glaze and kiln, hand-painting each bowl with love. I'm blessed!

ABOUT THE AUTHOR

Wendy Sosik is a certified mind/body coach, certified reiki practitioner, artist, and founder of LIVE AHA. She believes that every individual is capable of achieving peace and happiness at any age through clean, mindful living. Wendy's early training includes a fine arts degree from Montclair State University, as well as a degree from the Culinary Institute of America. She now devotes herself to inspiring others to accept themselves and live in the moment, to harness their powers of choice, and simply, to *wake up*. Included among Wendy's many-faceted professional roles are the wellness products that she designs via her company LIVE AHA. By offering healing jewelry, accessories, and Bowls For The Soul™, she endeavors to integrate meditation and mindfulness practice into an everyday lifestyle. Wendy also pays it forward, donating a portion of the proceeds to hand-picked charities that reflect her lifestyle and values.

From her home in Northwestern New Jersey, Wendy studies meditation, quantum science, and spirituality. She also enjoys cooking, painting, yoga, hiking, and traveling with her family.

www.ingramcontent.com/pod-product-compliance
Lightning Source LLC
LaVergne TN
LVHW010035070426
835510LV00006B/131